Putting Your Best Foot Forward
By Lewena Bayer

©Civility Experts Inc. Worldwide
All Rights Reserved 2020

Introduction
It's All About Respect

Everybody's talking about respect. What is respect anyway and how do you get it? It seems confusing at first but once you know what respect means, it's pretty easy to learn how to get it. Respect means showing care and consideration for others. The fastest and easiest way to get respect is to give respect. If others see you showing care and consideration towards them, they will probably start showing care and consideration towards you. Practicing good manners is one way of showing respect. Manners are a way of behaving, rules for being nice to each other. When we forget the rules, we make other people feel bad because they think we don't respect them. We all have lots of chances to show respect every day. For example:

- We can hold the door for someone when his or her hands are full.
- We can remember to say thank you when someone gives us something
- We can be patient when we're waiting in line and not push or shove.
- We can share our toys and treats with people who don't have any.
- We can include new people or little brothers and sisters when we play.

Showing respect for others makes it easier for people to live together and become friends. If you are kind and thoughtful to your friends, they will be kind and thoughtful to you too. Maybe they will invite you to parties. Maybe they'll help you clean up your room and maybe they'll share their new toys with you. It's very important to respect people.

Try to answer these questions out loud:

If there is a new boy in school and he doesn't know anyone.
I can show him respect by...

If I have a whole box of chocolate cookies and my friend doesn't have any.
I can show respect by...

So, let's go over it again. What do we call being nice to people, treating them well, and sharing with them?

It's just one word, RESPECT!

And how do we get other people to treat us with respect?
It's just two words, RESPECT PEOPLE!

Chapter 1
Smile! Make a Good First Impression

Have you ever been told to put your best foot forward? Do you know what that means? Well, we'll tell you. It means being the best you can be. Sort of like being on your very best behaviour all the time, and it's easier than you think. It's all about RESPECT.

A first impression is what you think of someone the first time you meet him or her. The way you introduce yourself, how you look, how you talk, your eye contact, your handshake, and whether or not you're smiling, helps people make a first impression of you. First impressions can last a long time and sometimes you never forget them. That's why it's so important to always put your best foot forward and remember your manners.

The first thing people see when they meet you is your face.

Try this. Look in a mirror. Now, show yourself these expressions:

- Curious
- Mad
- Bored
- Sour
- Worried
- Jealous

Now, how did you look? Did you like what you saw? Some of the faces weren't very friendly, were they? If you met someone with a mad face, or a sour face, or a jealous face, would you want to talk to them? We don't think we would.

Do you think it shows respect to meet people with a grouchy face? No way! Let's look in the mirror again with a happy, smiling expression. See? Now that's a friendly, happy face that other people will want to be around. People will respect you if you try to be happy and positive. You'll make a good first impression too.

Smile and the World Smiles With You
There's nothing in the world that makes people feel as good as a smile. Smiling is contagious, you know. That means "catchy." Try it. Walk around with a big smile pasted on your face and almost everybody who sees your smile will smile too. Smiling makes you feel good on the inside too.

Try smiling when you don't feel happy. You might be surprised at what happens. If you smile when you meet people, you'll make a good first impression.

Mirror, Mirror On the Wall
Do you remember what respect is? Showing care and consideration for other people, right? Well, it's important to show care and consideration for yourself too. That's called SELF-respect. If you respect yourself it means you care about how you look, talk, and act. Remember about first impressions? People will see your face and your clothes when they first meet you, so it's important to look good. How we look on the outside tells people how we feel about ourselves on the inside. If you see someone who didn't take a bath or brush their teeth and they were wearing wrinkled clothes, what would you think? Would you think they were tired, or lazy, or grouchy? Would you want to meet them? Probably not, that's why it's important to always brush your hair, take a bath, and make sure you have fresh breath. Don't forget to wear clean clothes too.

How to Introduce Yourself to Anyone
When people can see your smile, and how neat and clean you look

(they know you don't smell bad!), they'll want to talk to you. And if you see someone who looks clean and is smiling, you might want to talk to them too. This is called making an introduction. What do you do when you meet someone new? Say hello of course and tell them your name. Then ask their name. It's also polite to stand up when you meet someone, especially if they are older than you. If you are introduced to an older lady, you should call her Mrs. Unless she tells you Miss or Ms. If you meet a man, you should call him Mr. It's polite to always use the last name when speaking to adults – it's a way of showing respect. Remember to speak clearly and not too softly when you say your name.

Try introducing yourself to your parents or teacher. Remember, stand up, smile, and then say, hello (say the person's name, if it's a teacher remember to use Mrs. or Miss or Mr.), My name is (say your name). Try it a few times with different adults.

Now try it with someone your own age, but this time you can call whomever you meet by their first name because they're young too.

When you introduce yourself this way, you're making a good first impression. People will remember you and how polite you are, and they'll show you respect. Yes, adults can show respect to children too, especially when children show respect to them. This means the adults will treat you nicely, just like you treated them!

<u>Look Them In the Eyes</u>
When you meet someone new, you should look them in the eye when you say hello. This is called eye contact. Making eye contact is a very polite thing to do. You only have to look at their eyes long enough to see what colour they are. If you keep looking, people will think you're staring, and they might think you're rude.

Let's try an experiment: ask someone to talk with you and tell them not to look at you but to look around the room while they're talking. Now how does that make you feel? Like you're not important? Like they're not even interested in you? Try it again but with eye contact, remember not to stare, but look long enough so the other person knows that you care what they have to say.

Remember, if you listen to them, they'll listen to you.
Listening is good manners and it shows that you respect the person you are talking to.

No More Spaghetti Handshakes For Me
When you meet an adult, it's a good idea to shake hands. Now, why do that? Because that's a way to show them respect – plus, they'll be really impressed by you!

Did you ever touch someone's hand and it felt like a wet noodle? Well, that's "spaghetti" hands. Yuck! Make sure your hands are clean and dry when you shake someone's hand and don't keep your fingers all "loosey goosey" either. It's just as bad if you do the "bone crusher" when you meet someone. This means you squeeze their hand so tight they think their fingers might fall off. Not very nice. Practice with your mom or dad. Remember, no spaghetti fingers and no bone crusher. The best handshake is somewhere in the middle. Nice and firm. That's the way to do it. Nice and firm with a great big smile.

Let's review all the things we learned about making a good first impression:

1. Smile, it's "catchy."
2. Have self-respect. Make sure you look as good on the outside as you feel on the inside.
3. Introduce yourself – say hello and tell people your name.
4. Make eye contact. Don't let your eyes wander during a conversation.
5. Shake hands.

If you do all these things, people will want to be around you because they will see that you know that respect means always showing care and consideration for others.

Chapter 2
Conversations: How to Talk to People

Now that you've made a good first impression and introduced yourself to someone, what do you do next? Talk to them of course, have a conversation. It takes at least two people to have a conversation. When you are talking to someone, you might find out that they like the same things as you do or maybe that they live on your street. The only way to find out is to ask the other person questions about themselves. Don't forget to make eye contact with the person you are speaking to and just start asking him or her questions. It's very important to stop talking and listen after you have asked a question. Let the other person answer your questions and then they might want to ask you something. Listen while they talk and then answer them back.

Here are some questions you might ask someone you just met: have you seen the movie…? Do you like to eat…? What grade are you in? If you listen carefully to the answer, you will know what questions to ask next. Listening is very important.

<u>Listening First</u>

Did you ever try to talk to someone who was trying to talk to you at the same time? You probably couldn't understand each other, right? In a proper conversation, only one person talks at a time and the other person listens.

Listening shows that you respect the other person and think that what they have to say is important. After you have asked someone a question, you must listen to their answer. Listening is an important rule to remember about having a conversation.

No More Talkus Interruptus

Blah, blah, blah. That's all anybody hears when more than one person talks at a time. Everybody starts to talk louder too because they're trying to be heard over everyone else. You have to be very careful around "talkus interruptus" because it's contagious. The only way to stop it is by saying these magic words – "excuse me please." Imagine your best friend is talking to someone and you want to talk to them too. The polite thing to do is wait until they stop talking before you start talking. Even if you have something really exciting to say like maybe you just got a new bike, you have to wait until they're paying attention to you or they won't be listening anyway. Sometimes people say, "excuse me" and just start talking before anyone else has a chance to stop and listen. Even when you say, "excuse me", you still have to wait for people to stop talking and look at you so that you know it's your turn to talk.

Here's an experiment you can try: next time you are playing with a group of friends, stand quietly for a few minutes. Watch and listen. See if you can count how many times they interrupt each other when they are talking. You will probably notice that after one person starts to interrupt, everyone will get "talkus interruptus." Would you rather have a conversation with someone who shows respect for you by listening to what you have to say, or would you want to talk to someone with "talkus interruptus?" That's right! We'd rather talk to someone who listens too. Don't forget, it's all about showing respect.

Pardon Me?

When you're doing the talking, you want people to understand what you're saying, right? Try this tongue twister with a friend and see what you hear. Say this sentence really, really fast:

> *You're late Lily Langtry and languid lawlessness leads to lazy loathsome loafers.*

See? You can hardly say it and there is no way that anyone listening could understand what you said. They'll probably ask you to repeat yourself. So, let's try it again. This time speak slowly and clearly.

Much better! That's rule number three for having a conversation. Speak clearly and not too quickly. Do you remember rule number one? That's right – ask people questions about themselves. The second thing to do is to listen when someone else is talking. The third rule is to speak clearly and slowly. Now, what should you talk about when you're having a conversation?

Saying Nice Things
Remember when we were talking about respect and we said that respect means showing care and consideration for others? Well, this same rule applies to having a conversation.

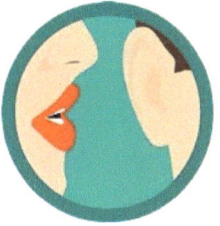

We can show respect by only saying nice things when we are having a conversation. Don't tell mean jokes or talk about other people. Have you ever heard of "gossip?" Gossip means spreading hurtful things about someone else.

It's not very respectful to gossip because it shows you do not care if someone's feelings get hurt. Think about how you would feel if someone said mean things about you. If someone tells you something that is not very nice, don't pass it on to another person. Instead, change the subject. Talk about the weather, something you've done lately or maybe your favourite book. If you don't gossip and say mean things, people will respect you because they will know they can trust you not to pass on hurtful things.

So, now you know how to get other people talking, what to talk about, and how to listen. Is there anything else? You bet!

Mind Your Please and Thank Yous

It's amazing how magical these words are. If you use them correctly, you will notice it's easier to get things done and people will like you. Do you remember what respect is? It's something you give to people and they give back to you. It's so easy, just three little words, please and thank you.

Always say please if you're asking for something and always say thank you when you receive something. Saying thank you shows that you appreciate what someone has given you or done for you. Do you know what appreciation means? Appreciation is understanding that someone has done something nice for you and showing them that you are thankful.

Stop for a minute and think about someone who you appreciate. Has someone done something nice for you lately? Something you can do to make people feel really appreciated is to write them a thank you card. It's especially nice to send thank you cards after birthdays and holidays.

Let's practice writing some cards. Find some paper and some crayons or markers. Fold the paper into a card. Make a design or picture on the front that shows what you appreciate or why you are happy. On the inside of the card write a note to the person you appreciate. The note should say:

Dear … (Write the person's name)
Thank you for … (Write what you are thankful for)
Love … (Write your name)

Here's an example of what a card would look like if you wanted to thank your grandmother for a beautiful sweater she made you:

Dear Grandma,
Thank you for the beautiful sweater. I will wear it when I go skating.
Love Joey

Boy, we sure have learned a lot about conversations. Do you remember the six important things to do when you have a conversation?

Let's review:
1. Ask people about themselves.
2. Listen when someone is talking to you.
3. Speak clearly and slowly.
4. Try not to be an "Interrupter".
5. Say nice things.
6. Remember please and thank you.

Chapter 3
Manners in Public Places: Going Out Into the World

Do you know what "public" means? It means people. Usually lots of people. Not like "private" which means just one or two or maybe a few people. It's important to know the difference because the rules for behaving are different when we're in public than when we're in private. In a private place, like when we're all alone in our room, we are allowed to make funny loud noises or leave a mess or sprawl out and take up lots of space. We can do all these things in private because it won't bother anyone else. It's different in public places though.

Look at the list of places and see if you can tell which ones are public places.

- School
- The grocery store
- The bathroom at home
- A restaurant
- The park
- The shopping mall
- Your bedroom
- The library

You did great! Now that you know the difference between public places and private places, can you guess how behaviours are different in public? Well, whenever you're in public, the secret is to think about how your actions will affect other people. Before you do anything, always ask yourself one question, "is what I'm doing a way to show respect to others?"

What's All the Noise About?
Did you ever go to the movies and someone behind you or beside you was talking during the show?

It was pretty hard to hear the movie, right? Maybe you had to ask the person to please be quiet because it seemed like they didn't notice that all the noise was bothering you. Whenever you're in a public place or there are  other people around, it's important to think about how loud you talk or even when you talk.

Doesn't it drive you crazy when you can't sleep because someone has their radio turned up too loud or they're making lots of noise early in the morning or late at night? Do you think it shows respect to make noise even if it bothers people? No way! Manners are about showing care and consideration for others and that means talking quietly and not making too much noise, so we don't bother other people, especially in public places. What will you ask yourself next time you go out in public? That's right, "is what I'm doing a way to show respect to others?"

<u>Things Have Feelings Too</u>
Something else to remember about public places is that the furniture and other things in public places are for everyone to use. So, we have to show care and consideration for these "things" too. Even if things don't belong to us, we should leave them the way we found them so that someone else can use them too. What if you went to a restaurant and someone who was there before you put their gum on the seat? That's right, you would probably not see it, and when you sat down you would have yucky gum all over your favourite pants.

What would happen if everyone who went to the park threw their garbage on the ground instead of putting it in the garbage can? Pretty soon the park would be full of litter and it wouldn't be nice to visit anymore, right? Do you think it shows respect to be careful with things that do not belong to us? Yes, it does! Stop and think for a minute about a time when someone broke something of yours. How did it make you feel?

Maybe you felt mad or sad, right? Maybe you even felt like they didn't respect you because they didn't take care of your things.
See, why it's important to show care and consideration for things, especially things that don't belong to us.

<u>Stop Crowding Me!</u>
What does public mean again? Lots of people, right? A lot of people in the same place at the same time. Did you ever hear someone say, "What a crowded place?" "Crowded" is what happens when lots of people are together in one space. It's very important for people to remember their manners and think about other people's space in public. What do you think would happen if you were on some crowded stairs at school and someone started pushing and shoving? You might fall down and get hurt right? What about when you are waiting in line to buy something and someone barges in front of you? Do you think they're invading your space? We do, and it doesn't feel good.

Here's an experiment, stand up, hold your arms out to your sides as high as your shoulders. Now, spin around once keeping your arms out. This usually how much space people like around them when they are in public places. We call it "personal space." So, in public places, we can show respect by showing care and consideration for other's personal space. This means not running or pushing or shoving or barging when space is crowded.

Look at the list of actions below and say out loud whether or not they are respectful things to do in public places. If they are not respectful things to do, say why.

- Stepping on people's feet
- Pushing in line
- Brushing up against people
- Walking in public places instead of running
- Reaching in front of people
- Barging in front of people

Very good and remember, whenever you're in public, always ask yourself, "is what I'm doing a way to show respect to others?" When we are in public places we should always think about how our actions will affect other people. It's all about respect. If everyone remembers their manners, it's easier for us all to get along in public places. Let's review three simple rules for behaving in public places like the grocery store, or the movie theatre, or restaurants, or the shopping centre:

1. Use "inside voices," quiet and calm voices for talking in public places. It's not polite to yell or talk loudly and make lots of noise because it bothers other people.
2. Show care and consideration for things that do not belong to you. Try not to litter and be careful not to break or ruin things that you use in public places.
3. Show respect for other people's space. Try not to crowd people or bump into them or accidentally push them. You should always walk in public places. People could get hurt if you run.

Chapter 4
Manners at School: How to Treat Your Teachers and Classmates

Did you know that most of us will spend at least thirteen years of our lives in school? That's a long time. If we put our best foot forward at school the time will go much faster and we will have lots of good memories. School is a public place, so we must follow all the rules we learned for behaving in public places. Do you remember the rules for behaving in public places? Use inside voices, show respect for other people's space and show care and consideration for things that do not belong to you. Very good! But, guess what? There are even more rules, special rules for school. These rules are about showing care and consideration for the people at school. Yes, you guessed it; the most important thing is respect. This means showing respect to your classmates and your teachers too.

Is Anybody Listening?

The easiest way to show respect to the teacher is to listen when they are talking. Let's pretend the teacher told you to go to the front of the class and tell everyone a story about your family.

Your family is important to you so you would probably be proud to tell everyone about them, right? Now, what if everyone in class ignored you and just kept on talking to each other. How would you feel? Would you feel mad or sad? Do you think that's how your teacher feels when no one listens? What would happen if you read comic books in class every day instead of listening to the teacher? That's right, you wouldn't learn anything and you wouldn't be able to move on to the next grade. There's always a reason for listening. Don't forget, RESPECT PEOPLE and when you're at school, this means the teacher.

Follow the Instructions
Listening is an important way to show the teacher respect. But there's more.

First, we must listen then we have to follow through and do what we hear. You know, the "instructions". Here's what I mean. If you hear the teacher say, "read chapter two," you must take your book home and read it, right? You can't just listen and then do nothing. Or if the teacher said, "Don't be late," you can't just listen to the words, you must pay attention and be on time. Maybe you've heard a teacher say, "How many times have I told you…"? This is what happens when people listen but don't follow through on what they hear. Listening to what the teacher says and following through on instructions shows that you respect yourself and the teacher. Just for fun try to think what would happen if you didn't leave when the teacher said, "class dismissed." What if you did nothing when your parents called you for dinner? Or, what if you heard someone say, "Turn right", but you decided to turn left instead? See, it's important to listen, but it's also important to follow through on what you hear.

Sharing is Caring
What about our classmates? We already know that showing care and consideration for other people is good manners. And we know that listening and following through on instructions is a way to show respect to the teacher. But what kind of things do we do to show respect to the other people at school, people like our classmates? Well, there are lots of things we can do. How about sharing? Or helping? What about trying only to say nice things?

Let's start with sharing. Sharing means you give something of yours to someone else, even though it means there will be less leftover for you. Sharing shows you care about other people. Think about a time when someone shared something with you. Didn't it make you feel special?

Put yourself in the situations below and think about what you could share:
- Your friend forgot to bring her lunch box to school and she is very hungry.
- You were the first person outside at recess and you got the best ball. Lots of kids didn't get a ball at all.
- Someone in your class cannot do their homework because his/her pencil broke.

Lend a Helping Hand
Sharing is one way to show you care about other people. Another way is helping. For example, if you fell down on the playground and cut yourself, you would like it if someone came to help you right? That's how you would know they care about you. What would you do if you saw someone spill a box of crayons? What about if your friend couldn't find a book she was looking for? Or, what if someone was lost? You would want to help them, right? Helping is a way of showing consideration. When you help people, you think about their feelings and want to make them feel better. Just like sharing, helping makes you feel good about yourself too.

Are you ready for a top-secret mission? Here it is. Try to lend a helping hand to someone every day for seven days in a row and see how good you feel afterward.

Gossip Hurts
There's another way to show respect for your classmates. Can you guess? Here's a hint.

We learned about it when we talked about making conversations. It was about gossip and telling mean jokes. Do you remember? Gossip means spreading hurtful things about someone else.

It's not very respectful to gossip because it shows you do not care if someone's feelings get hurt. Think about how you would feel if someone said mean things about you. Did anyone ever call you names? We can show respect for our classmates by only saying nice things. Even if someone is not very kind to you, maybe they are a bully or they hurt your feelings, it's better not to say mean things about them. Just remember, sometimes people say mean things because they don't like themselves very much, but if they see you act with respect, maybe they will try it too.

So, what did we learn about rules for behaving at a public place? Use inside voices, show respect for other people's space and show care and consideration for things that do not belong to you.

And what are the special rules for school?

1. Sharing
2. Helping
3. Saying nice things

Manners show you have respect, and when other people see you treat them with respect, they will treat you with respect too.

Chapter 5
Manners at Home: Respect Starts Here

Ever since you were very young your parents have been telling you to always say please and thank you, or to be nice to your little brother or sister, or to pick up your things. This is because manners begin at home and parents know that respect is important. Before we go out into the world, we learn how to give and get respect from our families. What can we do at home to show our parents or our brothers and sisters we respect them? Well, there are lots of simple things we can do every day. If you ever get stuck, try to ask yourself the same question you ask when you're doing something in a public place. Remember, "is what I'm doing showing respect for others?"

Watch Out For Cranky Pants
One important thing you can do to show your parents or brothers and sisters respect is to always talk to them in a friendly, calm voice.
Say nice things and wear a smile. Have you ever met a "cranky pants?" Sometimes when you feel grouchy, look in the mirror and you will see what a cranky pants looks like. No one wants to be around a grouchy person so try not to be moody and cranky with your family. Whining and shouting at them isn't very nice either. Whenever you think you might talk like a cranky pants,
remind yourself to wear a smile. It's almost magic, if you smile on the outside, you'll feel better on the inside and maybe you won't feel grouchy anymore. Besides, no one wants to be around a cranky grouch. Try to remember please and thank you too.

Respect Your Elders
What does it mean to respect your elders? I bet you've heard your parents say that lots of times. It means, show care and consideration to elders. Elders are people who are older than you, like adults.

It's important to listen to adults because they've lived longer and have lots of experience young people can learn from. Parents, especially, really appreciate it when young people respect them enough to listen and try to have a conversation now and then. Do you remember what appreciate means? If you forgot, look back in chapter two.

Here's something fun you can try: next time you have a question you don't have the answer to or maybe a problem you can't solve, go ask an elder person to help you. You could ask your parents, your grandparents, a teacher or even your brother and sister if they are older than you. I bet they have the answer you're looking for. And they probably have an interesting story to go with it too.

Here are some questions you could ask an elder person:

- What did you like to read when you were my age?
- Did anyone ever call you names when you went to school? What did you do?
- Did your parents make you do your homework?
- Who was your best friend in school?
- Can you remember your best ever summer holiday?

Hey, Be Careful With My Stuff
Another thing you can do to show respect is help around the house and do things without being asked.

Remember when we talked about showing care and considerations for things that don't belong to you? Well, that includes things that belong to your parents, like the TV, or the furniture or the house you live in. If everyone in the family helps take care of their own things and also helps take care of the things everyone shares, it will be easier to live together.

So, when your dad asks you to rake the back yard, what should you do? What about when your Mom tells you to clean up your room or fold the laundry?

Read through the list below. Can you say why your parents don't want you to do the following things?
- Don't put your shoes on the furniture
- Stop whining
- Don't act like a baby
- Stop fighting with your brother
- I don't want to have to tell you again
- You have to learn to take care of your things
- Don't look at me like that

Have you ever heard your parents say this kind of thing? If they do, it probably means you are forgetting your manners and they will remind you, so show more respect. Let's hope you don't hear these things very often.

So, you see, it's true; manners do start at home with our parents and families. What happens when you act like a grown-up and show your family respect? Well, they will treat you like a grown-up and shows you grown-up respect. Let's review the things we can do every day to show our parents or brothers and sisters respect:

1. Talk to them in calm, friendly voices. Try not to yell or whine at them.
2. Listen to them and have a conversation now and then.
3. Do things without being asked and help take care of your things as well as things everyone shares.

If we remember these easy rules and learn to treat our family with respect, we will know how to act when we get out into the world and meet people who might be different than our family.

Chapter 6
How to Deal With Someone Who Is Different From You

Now that we understand what respect is, we know that if we show care and consideration for other people, they will show us care and consideration. It's easy to be nice to our family and friends but what about strangers and people we don't know. Sometimes it's hard to be nice to someone who looks different than we do. It's important to remember that we probably look different to them too.

Everybody deserves respect even if they have different hair, different clothes, speak a different language or celebrate different holidays than we do. Some people might even eat different food than we do. Even if a lot of things seem different about someone, just remember, they're a person too. And just like you, they might feel scared or shy or nervous when they see someone different… like you. But they will probably show you care and consideration if you show them care and consideration.

What About the Purple People?
When I was young, there used to be a funny song on the radio. The words went something like this:

"It was a one-eyed, one-horned, flying purple people eater."

Boy, I don't know what I'd do if I ever saw one of those. You would probably never run into a flying purple people eater or even a purple person. But you might run into someone who looks different. Maybe they have different colour skin or they're really tall or really skinny. Maybe they're in a wheelchair or only have one arm. Maybe you'll meet someone who has a learning difficulty and can't speak as well as you or maybe you'll even meet someone who is visually impaired. What would you do?

Well, this is an easy one. There is only one rule for how to behave with people who seem different than you are, don't do anything. Anything different that is. Remember it's always about respect. So, just treat someone who seems different exactly the same way you treat everyone else, with respect. Maybe they have special needs like an older person sometimes has to go slow or a hard-of-hearing person might talk with sign language. It doesn't matter. Just do what you would always do. Don't forget, you always want to make a good first impression.

Stop Staring

So, how do you make a good first impression? Smile, make eye contact and introduce yourself. If you notice something different about someone when you meet them, like maybe they have just one arm or maybe they walk with a cane, try not to stare. Staring makes people feel uncomfortable and no one likes to feel uncomfortable. Just remember, if someone looks different to you, you probably look different to them too, and you don't want to be stared at.

It's not polite to ask about something different either, but you can talk about it if the other person brings up the subject when you're having a conversation. It's important to think about how your actions affect other people. Remember? We learned that when we were talking about how to behave in public places. For example, if you had to be on crutches because you broke your leg, how would you feel if someone laughed at you or tried to trip you? You would probably feel very sad, right? And remember what we learned about always saying nice things? Even if someone seems different, we shouldn't say mean things about them. We should always treat people with respect, the same as we want them to treat us with respect.

Wouldn't life be boring if we were all exactly the same?

Can you imagine what it would be like if we were all the same? Let's pretend. Imagine that everyone in the whole world looks the same as you. Imagine everyone talks the same and looks the same.

Hey, wait a minute, where's your mom, what about your dad? It would be pretty hard to find special people if everyone was the same wouldn't it? The world would sure be boring. Thank goodness we're all different. Isn't it great that we're all people but we're all special in some way? It's being different that makes us special. Different doesn't just mean how we look or talk, it's more than that. Different means how we do things, what we like, where we live, what we eat, how we dress, and lots of other things. It's what's different about you that makes you special. Everybody has something. Think about people you know. What's special about them? Every time you meet or see someone who is different than you in some way try to find out what is it that makes them special. Different just means special and we're all just people, right?

Put Yourself in Their Shoes
Let's stop for a minute and think about a time when someone treated you badly.

Maybe they stared at you or laughed at you because they thought you were different. How did that make you feel? Not very good, right? It probably hurt your feelings. Saying mean things is not a way to show care and consideration for other people. Always think about how you might feel if you were the other person and treat them the way you would want to be treated.

Here's an example, pretend you're in gym class and everyone is playing baseball. When it is your friend's turn to pitch the ball, he tries, but it doesn't go very far so everyone gets mad at him and starts calling him a "bellyitcher" because he's a bad pitcher. Would you make fun of him too? What if that was you? What if everyone was calling you names? You would feel awful, right? Yes! So, if you wouldn't like people to do something to you, you shouldn't do it to them.

What Would You Do?
Remember when we were talking about how to show respect to your classmates? That's right, we said to always try to share, help and say nice things. Maybe some of your classmates aren't your best friends but you still show them respect because you have to go to school together, right? Well, it's kind of the same when you're out in the world with strangers and people who seem different than you. Maybe you don't know everyone really well, but you still have to live in the world together, so it's important to show them respect. Why? So, they'll show you respect. So, the same special rules for behaving with classmates apply to behaving with people who seem different. Always try to share. Lend a helping hand and only say nice things. Let's try it.

Put yourself in the situations below and say out loud what you would do.
- What if you do if you were introduced to a person with a different colour skin than you have?
- What if an older person with a cane fell on the sidewalk?
- What if someone didn't have any cool clothes to wear to school?
- What if you saw someone who talked funny?
- What if you met a little boy who couldn't play outside because he was sick?

The world is a pretty big place and there are many, many different people. It's our differences that make us special though and we should treat everyone with respect. Always treat people who seem different the same as everybody else and try to share, lend a helping hand, and say nice things.

Conclusion
The Respect Roundup

Good job! You are almost a manners expert now. You have lots of new manners rules you can teach your friends. Let's review what we learned and then you can try the etiquette quiz. Good Luck!

Review

1. Respect is showing care and consideration for others.
2. Self-respect is showing care and consideration for myself.
3. You can make a good impression if you remember to smile, keep yourself neat and clean, introduce yourself, look people in the eye, and shake hands.
4. When having a conversation, ask people about themselves, speak clearly and slowly, and listen.
5. In public places, use "inside voices" and remember to respect other people's space.
6. Show care and consideration for things that don't belong to you.
7. Listen to your teacher and follow instructions.
8. Share with your classmates, help them, and always say nice things.
9. Manners begin at home. If you learn to show respect to your family, you will know how to act when you get out into the world.
10. People who are different than you deserve respect too. It's our differences that make us special and you should treat people the way you want them to treat you.

The Etiquette Quiz

Take the quiz below. Say out loud if the statement is true or false. Then turn to the very last page and check how many questions you answered correctly.

1. If I'm tired, it's okay to wear sloppy clothes.

2. It's okay to scream and yell and run in public places.

3. If other people talk about me, it's okay to talk about them.

4. I can wear my dirty shirt to go to my Grandma's.

5. I should shake hands with people when I first meet them.

6. When I answer the phone and it's for my mother, I should yell for her to come to the phone.

7. The first thing I should do when someone's talking is to interrupt them.

8. If I'm at a party and people are eating turnips, but I don't like them, I should make a face and say, "gross!"

9. Having good manners gives you self-esteem.

10. If you meet someone with purple hair, you should tell them they look stupid.

Here are the answers to the quiz:

1. False
2. False
3. False
4. False
5. True
6. False
7. False
8. False
9. True
10. False

www.ingramcontent.com/pod-product-compliance
Lightning Source LLC
LaVergne TN
LVHW010035070426
835510LV00006B/132